Date: 12/14/11

J 581 WAD
Wade, Mary Dodson.
Plants live everywhere! /

PLANTS LIVE
EVERYWHERE!

Mary Dodson Wade

Series Science Consultant:
Mary Poulson, Ph.D.
Associate Professor of Plant Biology
Department of Biological Sciences
Central Washington University
Ellensburg, WA

Series Literacy Consultant:
Allan A. De Fina, Ph.D.
Past President of the New Jersey Reading Association
Chairperson, Department of Literacy Education
New Jersey City University
Jersey City, NJ

CONTENTS

WORDS TO KNOW

Arctic (ARK tik)—A very cold area of the world close to the North Pole.

mild (MY uld)—Not hot or cold.

shade (SHAYD)—A place that is not sunny.

PARTS OF A PLANT

flower

leaf

stem

roots

WHERE DO PLANTS GROW?

Plants grow in many places.

They grow in forests, parks, and yards.

They grow in fields and next to roads.

They grow in lakes and deserts.

All plants need sunlight, water, air, and food.

Water lilies grow in ponds.

WHAT PLANTS GROW IN THE ARCTIC?

The **Arctic** is an icy cold place for most of the year. During the short summers, small plants make flowers, or bloom.

Lupines (LOO pyns) bloom in the Arctic in Canada.

Bright yellow Arctic poppies bloom in the summer.

A blue agave (uh GAH vee) plant grows in the Texas desert.

WHAT PLANTS GROW IN THE DESERT?

The desert is hot and dry. Desert plants do not have big leaves like some plants. Big leaves let water escape from the plant. Desert plants, like the cactus, hold water in their stems.

Some desert plants have thorns to keep animals from eating them.

cactus

9

WHAT PLANTS GROW IN THE RAIN FOREST?

Rain forests are warm, rainy places. They are crowded with many, many plants! Some of the trees grow very tall. Other plants grow under the tall trees.

Some plants, like bromeliads (broh MEE lee ads), grow on trees.

Vines climb up the tall trees to reach
the sunshine.

WHAT PLANTS GROW IN THE WOODLAND FOREST?

Woodland forests grow where the weather is **mild**—not too hot or too cold. Trees and bushes grow during the warm summer. Many forest plants, such as oak trees, lose their leaves and sleep during the winter. Pine trees stay green all year.

WHAT PLANTS GROW IN THE GRASSLANDS?

Grasses cover the grasslands. They do not need as much water as trees. Grassland plants do not have bright, showy flowers. The flowers may be fluffy and brown.

◄ Oklahoma grasslands

grass flowers

WHAT PLANTS GROW IN THE WATER?

Some plants live in water. Water lilies have long stems to reach the mud at the bottom of a pond. Duckweed floats in lakes, streams, and ponds. Marsh grass grows along rivers.

leaf

stem

This photo of water lilies was taken underwater.

marsh grass

Elm trees were planted in a line on this street.

WHAT PLANTS GROW IN THE CITY?

In the city, elm trees grow tall and give **shade**. Bushes, grass, and flowers are planted around buildings. People hang baskets filled with flowers. They visit city parks that are filled with plants. People like to have plants near them.

WHICH PLANT NEEDS MORE
WATER?

You will need:
* ✳ small cactus plant in a pot
* ✳ small potted plant like a tomato plant or a mum.
* ✳ water
* ✳ sunny window

Make sure both plants are about the same size and are in the same kind of soil.

1. Water both plants to make the soil damp.

2. Place both plants in a window that gets lots of sun.

3. Do not water the plants again for two weeks.

After two weeks, look at the plants. Feel the soil. Is it dry? Have the plants changed in any way? Which plant seems to need more water?

The cactus is a desert plant. Cactus plants can go without water for a long time. Other types of plants need water more often.

LEARN MORE

BOOKS

Dell, Pamela. *Ocean Plants*. Minneapolis: Bridgestone Books, 2005.

Kalman, Bobbie, and Rebecca Sjonger. *Plants in Different Habitats*. New York: Crabtree, 2006.

Riley, Peter. *Plants*. Milwaukee, Wis.: Gareth Stevens, 2004.

Spilsbury, Louise, and Richard Spilsbury. *What Is a Plant?* Chicago: Heinemann Library, 2006.

WEB SITES

Enchanted Learning. *Habitats/Biomes.*
   <http://www.enchantedlearning.com/biomes/>

University of Illinois. *The Great Plant Escape.*
   <http://www.urbanext.uiuc.edu/gpe>

U.S. Department of Agriculture. *Sci4Kids.* **"Plants."**
   <http://www.ars.usda.gov/is/kids>

INDEX

Enslow Elementary, an imprint of Enslow Publishers, Inc.
Enslow Elementary® is a registered trademark of
Enslow Publishers, Inc.

Copyright © 2009 by Enslow Publishers, Inc.

Library of Congress Cataloging-in-Publication Data

Wade, Mary Dodson.
    Plants live everywhere! / Mary Dodson Wade.
        p. cm. — (I like plants!)
    Summary: "Information about plants living in different
    habitats for young readers"—Provided by publisher.
    Includes bibliographical references and index.
    ISBN-13: 978-0-7660-3155-5 (library ed.)
    ISBN-10: 0-7660-3155-1 (library ed.)
        1. Phytogeography—Juvenile literature. I. Title.
QK101.W23 2009
581.9—dc22   2007039457

ISBN-13: 978-0-7660-3615-4 (paperback)
ISBN-10: 0-7660-3615-4 (paperback)

Printed in the United States of America
052010 Lake Book Manufacturing, Inc., Melrose Park, IL

10 9 8 7 6 5 4 3 2

Every effort has been made to locate all copyright holders of
material used in this book. If any errors or omissions have
occurred, corrections will be made in future editions of this
book.

To Our Readers: We have done our best to make sure all
Internet Addresses in this book were active and appropriate
when we went to press. However, the author and the publisher
have no control over and assume no liability for the material
available on those Internet sites or on other Web sites they may
link to. Any comments or suggestions can be sent by e-mail to
comments@enslow.com or to the address on the back cover.

♻ Enslow Publishers, Inc., is committed to printing our books on
recycled paper. The paper in every book contains 10% to 30% post-
consumer waste (PCW). The cover board on the outside of each book
contains 100% PCW. Our goal is to do our part to help young people and the environment too!

Note to Parents and Teachers: The *I Like Plants!* series supports the
National Science Education Standards for K–4 science. The Words to
Know section introduces subject-specific vocabulary words, including
pronunciation and definitions. Early readers may need help with
these new words.

Photo Credits: Enslow Publishers, Inc., p. 23; iStockphoto.com:
© Jorge Salcedo, p. 19, © Malcolm Romain, p. 3, © Sergei
Sverdelov, p. 13, © YinYang, p. 20 (mum); Minden Pictures: © Frans
Lanting, pp. 11, 16, © Jim Brandenburg, p. 12, © Louis Gagnon,
p. 5, © Pete Cairns, p. 17, © Tui De Roy, p. 10; Photo Researchers,
Inc.: James Steinberg, p. 14, Larry Landolfi, p. 8, Nigel Cattlin,
p. 4, Stephen J. Krasemann, p. 6; Shutterstock, pp. 1, 2, 18, 20
(cactus); Visuals Unlimited: © Gerald and Buff Corsi, p. 7, © Glenn
Oliver, p. 9, © Nigel Cattlin, p. 15.

Cover Photo: © Louis Gagnon/Minden Pictures

Enslow Elementary
an imprint of
Enslow Publishers, Inc.
40 Industrial Road
Box 398
Berkeley Heights, NJ 07922
USA

http://www.enslow.com